ATLANTA

The Delaplaine
2022 Long Weekend Guide

Andrew Delaplaine

NO BUSINESS HAS PAID A SINGLE PENNY OR GIVEN *ANYTHING* TO BE INCLUDED IN THIS BOOK.

Contributors
James Cubby

Gramercy Park Press
New York – London - Paris

Please submit corrections, additions or comments to
andrewdelaplaine@mac.com

ATLANTA
The Delaplaine
Long Weekend Guide

TABLE OF CONTENTS

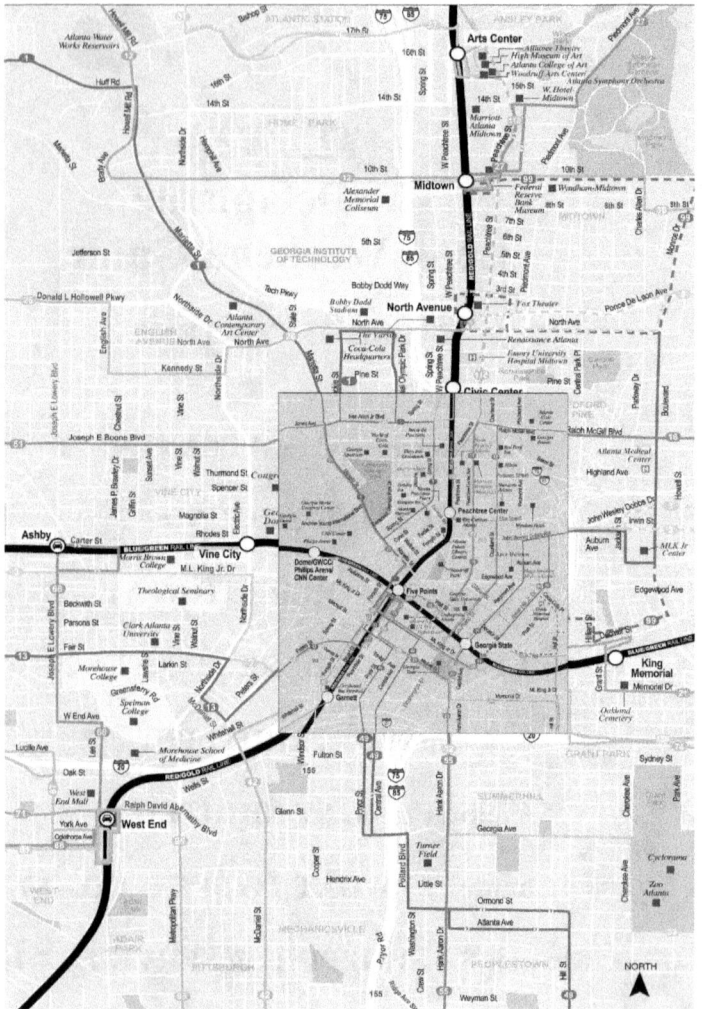

Chapter 1
WHY ATLANTA?

Hotlanta?

There's no city that can lay a greater claim to represent what used to be termed the "New South" than the city of Atlanta.

It was burned down in the Civil War (or as my Fifth Grade teacher Mrs. McCutcheon sternly reminded me in the 1960s, "the War of Northern Aggression") during General Sherman's famous "March to the Sea," and to this day remains the only major American city completely annihilated by war. Sherman burned all the railroad depots, uprooted the tracks, burned every business to the ground and for good measure to show that he meant it, burned down two-thirds of the private homes.

Perhaps that's why Atlanta's resurgence so captured the imagination. When it became the home of the Civil Rights Movement in the 1960s, led by Dr. Martin Luther King, Jr., Atlanta took on yet another level of symbolic importance.

Non-natives are familiar if not with Atlanta itself, then surely with its huge airport. Hartsfield-Jackson International Airport is the world's busiest airport, with more than 88 million annual passengers. (By comparison, London's Heathrow only has 64 million people passing through it.)

Hosting the Olympics in 1996 gave Atlanta an international profile and drove many upgrades to the city. The **MARTA** public transport system is efficient and a major addition to the city's infrastructure. The **World Congress Center** was built to attract the most desirable convention business and it has worked.

It's "Hotlanta" all right.

Chapter 2
GETTING AROUND

    Atlanta is unique in that it has 3 separate skylines. Downtown, Midtown and Buckhead each has its own skyline that would make an admirable statement by itself.

    DOWNTOWN consists of **Five Points**, **Centennial Park**, Sweet Auburn, Castleberry Hill and the **Hotel District**. This is where you'll find the state Capitol, City Hall, the **CNN Center**, **Georgia Aquarium** and the **World of Coca-Cola Museum**. While most tourists congregate in Downtown, I advise you not to make the same mistake. Locals tend to disappear from Downtown after dark, so you should follow them to one of the many completely different neighborhoods they go to at night.

MIDTOWN is the area just north of Downtown. It's a major business and residential district with big buildings and a concentrated nightlife section. Piedmont Park, the Woodruff Arts Center and the Georgia Tech campus are located here.

BUCKHEAD is a few miles north of Midtown. It's a popular business and nightlife area. Buckhead is surrounded by neighboring **Brookwood Hills**, as well as Peachtree Battle, **Lindbergh Center**, and the Governor's Mansion.

EAST ATLANTA, also called **East Atlanta Village,** has great neighborhoods with beautiful homes, some of the best bars and restaurants in town and a bustling shopping scene. It's a gentrifying area, but it's cool. It's south of I-20 and Moreland Avenue.

INMAN PARK, **LITTLE FIVE POINTS, CANDLER PARK** are clustered together and are a center for nightlife and no-hype restaurants favored by the locals. Little Five Points has great murals you'll see as you walk around.

VIRGINIA-HIGHLANDS is nearby—it has some of the nicer housing in the area.

BY CAR
As anyone who's been here knows, downtown traffic in Atlanta is a nightmare at rush hour. If you're only on a short visit, forego getting a rental car and rely on cabs or MARTA to get around. I have pretty much stopped using cabs, except in places where **Uber** and **Lyft** aren't operating.

If you still don't have these apps, you gotta get them. If you're just signing up, use my codes and I'll get a free ride and you'll get discounts as well.
UBER INVITE CODE – **andrewd145**
LYFT INVITE CODE – **andrew163551**

BY FOOT
Once you're in any given neighborhood, walking is just fine. Shops, restaurants and bars are usually clustered together, so whether you're in Inman Park, Little Five Points, Midtown, Downtown, etc., you'll be OK. It's getting between these little neighborhoods that presents a challenge. This is where you'll want to grab a taxi or use MARTA.

MARTA
The Metropolitan Atlanta Rapid Transit Authority, www.itsmarta.com, runs the trains and bus lines and does a very good job. (Various passes, called **Breeze Cards**, are available, depending on how long you're in town.)

TAXI
In dense areas like Downtown, cabs are easy to get. But you can always call ahead: Checker Cab: 404-351-1111. www.atlantacheckercab.com

Chapter 3
WHERE TO STAY

ARTMORE HOTEL
1302 West Peachtree St, NW, 404-876-6100
www.artmorehotel.com
NEIGHBORHOOD: Midtown
This unique Midtown boutique hotel delivers
personalized service. Once you get past the

inauspicious façade, you'll discover an historic landmark dating from 1924 that has been restored beautifully. It was an old apartment building that still has lovely Spanish design themes and an offbeat charm. In good weather, you can join the other guests as they sip cocktails around a fountain that also has a fire pit. Has several split-level suites. Located across the street from MARTA, High Museum, Alliance Theater and the Atlanta Symphony Orchestra. This is a fine option if you don't want to stay in one of the big chain hotels.

THE ELLIS
176 Peachtree St. NW, 404-523-5155
www.ellishotel.com
NEIGHBORHOOD: Downtown
Charming Downtown property in a building dating back to 1913. It was reopened in 2007 after a thorough renovation costing over $25 million. Nothing fusty about it; completely modern and sleek. Bamboo paneling in the rooms and limestone in the baths. The **Terrace Bistro** makes a good spot for people-watching as you overlook Peachtree Street. (It also has very good food from local farms.)

FOUR SEASONS

75 14th St. NE, 404-881-9898

www.fourseasons.com/atlanta/

NEIGHBORHOOD: Midtown

Offering typical Four Seasons luxurious accommodations and service. This location boasts 244 ultra-spacious guest rooms including 18 luxury suites. Amenities available: spa treatments, indoor saline lap pool, and Atlanta's most luxurious fitness center.

GEORGIAN TERRACE

659 Peachtree St NE, 404-897-1991

thegeorgianterrace.com

NEIGHBORHOOD: Midtown, Business & Cultural District

This gorgeous old 326-room Beaux Arts hotel (dating

from 1911) was the site of the premiere gala for *Gone With the Wind* in 1939. Listed on the National

Register of Historic Places, this hotel is known for its dramatic vistas and excellent Southern service. Located just a few steps from the historic Fox Theatre, where "Gone With the Wind" premiered. Clark Gable actually stayed here. If you're not staying here, at least stop in to enjoy a drink at the elegant high-ceilinged bar with its charming crown molding. Amenities include a rooftop pool, a friendly bar, and a sexy speakeasy in the basement. Some of their rooms are part of the "Southern Living Hotel Collection," a list of 4 and 5-star independent resorts carefully vetted and approved by "Southern Living" magazine.

HIGHLAND INN
644 North Highland Ave., 404-874-5756

www.thehighlandinn.com/
NEIGHBORHOOD: Poncey/Highland
Historic hotel, built in 1927, with great service. Basic but comfortable accommodations and surprisingly affordable. Great location.

HOTEL INDIGO
683 Peachtree St. NE, 404-874-9200
www.hotelindigo.com
NEIGHBORHOOD: Midtown
What used to be an old Days Inn has been beautifully transformed into a chic boutique hotel property. (About a mile north of the Aquarium.)

MICROTEL INN & SUITES
1840 Corporate Blvd., 404-410-0312
www.microtelinn.com
NEIGHBORHOOD: Buckhead
Out in Buckhead, this is a super choice for families. This budget property has a microwave in the room, a refrigerator and free Continental breakfast.

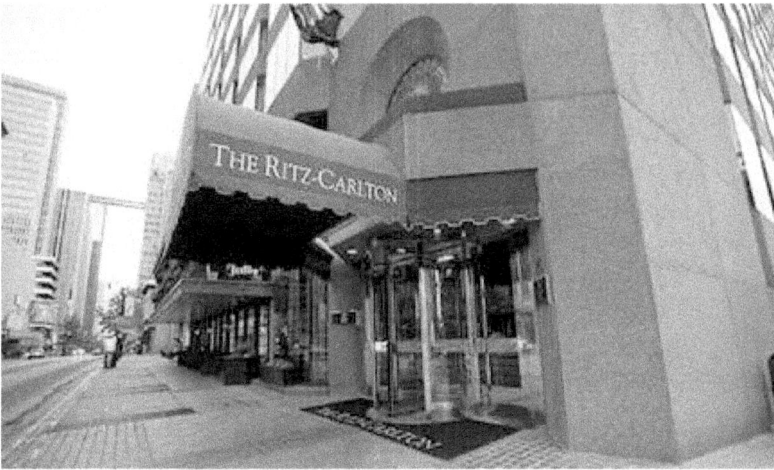

RITZ-CARLTON
181 Peachtree St. NE, 404-659-0400
www.ritzcarlton.com
NEIGHBORHOOD: Downtown
This Ritz-Carlton is located in the heart of Atlanta and features beautiful interiors. This location has 444 elegantly appointed rooms, including 22 suites with bay window views of the downtown Atlanta skyline. Amenities include: luxury hotel lobby bar, Wireless High-Speed Internet Access (daily fee applies), and iPod docking stations.

ST. REGIS
88 W. Paces Ferry Rd., 404-563-7900
www.stregisatlanta.com/
NEIGHBORHOOD: Buckhead
The St. Regis has a great environment that is a must see. It's the tops for luxury and grandeur with its majestic staircases, crystal chandeliers. It's got a little bit of everything: great hotel service (Egyptian cotton

sheets on the beds, marble baths), a wine bar, **Astor Court**, afternoon tea, and a great bar modeled after the famous King Cole Bar in New York's St. Regis. Only the mural behind the bar here is not of King Cole, but of a phoenix rising from the ashes, which is a motif extensively displayed in Atlanta. If you order the "Southern" cocktail, you'll be getting their bespoke bourbon made for the hotel by Woodford Reserve. The next-day suit service is handled by the famous local menswear designer, Sid Mashburn. Since Atlanta is the center of a booming film industry thanks to the state's attractive tax incentive program that lures Hollywood productions to Georgia, this place is a hotbed of celebrities.

STONEHURST PLACE B&B
923 Piedmont Ave. NE, 404-881-0722
www.stonehurstplace.com
NEIGHBORHOOD: Midtown

Built in 1896, this is Atlanta's only eco-friendly, luxury Bed & Breakfast with an excellent view of Piedmont Park (what Central Park is to Manhattan, Piedmont is to Atlanta). A beautiful B&B featuring only 6 lovely renovated rooms in a variety of sizes, some with queen beds, vintage baths and fireplaces, others with king beds, marble floors, spa tubs, and walk-in showers. Attentive service. You can walk through the garden where you'll find many of the plants labeled. Something I like to do at twilight is to sit on the front porch and watch the city lights come on. Amenities include: gourmet breakfast, hand-ironed luxury linens, iPod docking stations, wireless Internet and on-site parking. Non-smoking venue.

W ATLANTA
45 Ivan Allen Jr. Blvd., 404-582-5800
www.watlantadowntown.com
NEIGHBORHOOD: Downtown

The lush W Atlanta offers a convenient location near Atlanta nightlife and attractions like the Georgia Aquarium, Centennial Olympic Park and the Georgia Dome. Amenities include: cozy Living Room bar, outdoor heated pool, state-of-the-art fitness center, Bliss Spa and private heliport.

W ATLANTA
3377 Peachtree Rd. NE, 678-500-3100
www.watlantabuckhead.com
NEIGHBORHOOD: Buckhead

W Atlanta, an upscale boutique hotel, offers a prime location near shopping, fine dining and entertainment. Buckhead's hippest rooftop bar, Whiskey Blue Atlanta, is located on the 12th floor. On site restaurant, Cook Hall, offers contemporary cuisine. Other amenities include: fully equipped fitness center, WET deck, and infinity-edge pool overlooking Peachtree Road. Luxurious rooms come with the latest technology like Wi-Fi.

WALDORF ASTORIA
3376 Peachtree Rd. NE, 404-995-7500
https://waldorfastoria3.hilton.com
NEIGHBORHOOD: Buckhead
Five-star luxury hotel features beautiful rooms, superb restaurant and an elegant spa. Offering 117 luxurious rooms with large bathrooms and 10 spacious suites with balconies. Located close to the Atlanta Botanical Garden, Georgia Aquarium and the High Museum of Art.

WESTIN PEACHTREE PLAZA
210 Peachtree St. NW, 404-659-1400
www.westinpeachtreeplazaatlanta.com
NEIGHBORHOOD: Downtown
One of Atlanta's skyline icons, the revolving Sun Dial Restaurant tops off this 73-story hotel. Located downtown near all the attractions and attached to AmericasMart. 1,068 rooms featuring floor-to-ceiling windows, the Westin Heavenly Bed, marble Heavenly Bath, and cutting-edge entertainment.

THE WHITLEY
3434 Peachtree Rd. NE, 404-237-2700
https://www.marriott.com
NEIGHBORHOOD: Buckhead
This property offers the hospitality and sophistication that one would expect from a Ritz-Carlton. This location has 510 elegantly appointed guest rooms including 56 suites featuring bay window views of the city's skyline. Ritz-Carlton boasts intimate service and luxurious accommodations, an exclusive **Spa**, exquisite dining.

Chapter 4
WHERE TO EAT

In "The Virginia House-Wife" by Mary Randolph, published in 1824, you'll find the first recipe for Southern Fried Chicken:

"Cut [the chicken] up as for the fricassee, dredge the pieces well with flour, sprinkle them with salt, put them into a good quantity of boiling lard, and fry them a light brown."

Can't get much simpler than that.

And yet such simplicity has allowed the term "fried chicken" to be interpreted in hundreds of thousands of different ways, almost all of them perfectly wonderful, to my mind, having been raised in South Carolina on a plantation.

With slaves adding spices redolent of their West African homeland, the variations on the theme exploded, and continue to unfold today.

Even in the finest of fine restaurants, you'll find world-renowned chefs unable to shake the urge to put their signature touch to this most American of all-American foods.

O4W PIZZA
3117 Main St, Duluth, 678-587-5420
www.o4wpizza.com
CUISINE: American (New), Diners
DRINKS: Full Bar
SERVING: Lunch, Dinner, Brunch
PRICE RANGE: $$
NEIGHBORHOOD: Duluth
This pizzeria (Jersey-style) is known for its "Grandma pizza"- a 16-inch square Margherita-style pizza cooked in a cast-iron pan made with mozzarella and marinara sauce. Of the 100 other dishes & pizzas on this menu are standouts like Duck prosciutto, and cashew cheese margarita pies. Gluten-free pizza also available. Many times before we've called a place "no frills," this is perhaps even more accurately described as "zero frills." A few picnic tables outside and a bare-bones counter inside. Bu the food's great!

8 ARM
710 Ponce De Leon Ave NE, 470-875-5856
www.8armatl.com

CUISINE: American (New), Breakfast & Brunch
DRINKS: Wine Bar
SERVING: Breakfast, Lunch, & Dinner (hours vary, so check web site)
PRICE RANGE: $$
NEIGHBORHOOD: Virginia Highland
Casual café (bright, simple, cheerful, with those terrible clunky metal stools that are so uncomfortable) serving New American fare for lunch (mostly vegetarian) and specialties for dinner. Pork Tostada, Crispy Duck Breast (with ricotta squash and confit potatoes), Butternut Squash Quiche; Fried Green Tomatoes. Great brunch selection. Menu changes often. Communal seating outside (dog friendly).

ALMA COCINA
191 Peachtree Street NE, 404-968-9662
www.alma-atlanta.com
CUISINE: Latin American, Brazilian, Mexican
DRINKS: Full Bar
SERVING: Lunch, Dinner
PRICE RANGE: $$
NEIGHBOROOD: Downtown
Serving up contemporary Latin and Mexican cuisine mixing fresh ingredients and traditional regional influences. Delicious menu selections like "Fried Avocado" tacos and "Chicken Mole Oaxaca." They have interesting twists on classic recipes. The Fried Avocado tacos, for instance, are served with a poblano pesto instead of salsa. They go to great lengths to make sure everything here is as good as it can possibly be. They even go down to Mexico to buy their tequila by the keg. Innovative cocktails.

ARIA
490 E Paces Ferry Rd NE, Atlanta, 404-233-7673
www.aria-atl.com
CUISINE: American (New)
DRINKS: Full Bar
SERVING: Dinner, Closed Sundays
PRICE RANGE: $$$
NEIGHBORHOOD: Buckhead
Award-winning eatery offering a menu of
sophisticated dishes in a simple setting with bench
seating along a wall with mirrors lining the wall
above on a dark gray wall. Nice bar for cocktails.
Favorites: Butter Braised Lobster, Rainbow Trout and
Beef Short Ribs. Specialty desserts. Nice selection of
wines and crafted cocktails.

ATKINS PARK RESTAURANT
794 N Highland Ave. NE, 404-876-7249
www.atkinspark.com
CUISINE: American (Traditional)
DRINKS: Full Bar
SERVING: Lunch, Dinner, Brunch
PRICE RANGE: $$
NEIGHBORHOOD: Virginia Highlands
Atlanta's oldest restaurant and bar located in the
historical Atkins Park Tavern. This is a great dining
spot for families. Great food and atmosphere.

ANTICO PIZZA
1093 Hemphill Ave NW, 404-724-2333
www.littleitalia.com
CUISINE: Pizza

DRINKS: No Booze
SERVING: Lunch, Dinner
PRICE RANGE: $$
NEIGHBOROOD: Westside/Home Park
Great pizza, some say the best in Atlanta. This Neapolitan-style pizzeria is not only a local's favorite but its pizzas have been ranked among the top five in the country. Usually crowded but worth the wait.

BACCHANALIA
1460 Ellsworth Industrial Blvd, 404.365.0410 ext. 2
www.starprovisions.com
CUISINE: American
DRINKS: Full Bar
SERVING: Dinner
PRICE RANGE: $$$$
NEIGHBORHOOD: West Midtown
One of Atlanta's most celebrated restaurants serving great food with a fabulous wait staff and excellent wine selection. Chefs Quatrano and Clifford Harrison offer a seasonal menu with many items coming from their farm. Way back in 1993 when they opened, they were among the first to bring the farm-to-table philosophy to Atlanta. Lucky for them, they had a farm! A lot of chefs with their own celebrated eateries in Atlanta started off in the kitchen here, so that tells you how important this place is in the firmament of Atlanta culinary traditions.

BANTAM + BIDDY
1544 Piedmont Ave, 404-254-4601
www.bantamandbiddy.com
CUISINE: American (New); Diner

DRINKS: Full Bar
SERVING: Lunch, Dinner, Brunch
PRICE RANGE: $$
NEIGHBORHOOD: in town
Located in Ansley Mall, Bantam + Biddy offers a casual, family-friendly setting featuring regional, all-natural and pastured poultry. Get the crispy skin rotisserie bird served with different sauces.

BARCELONA
240 N. Highland Ave. NE, 404-589-1010
www.barcelonawinebar.com/
CUISINE: American; Spanish
DRINKS: Full Bar
SERVING: lunch / dinner
PRICE RANGE: $$$
NEIGHBORHOOD: Inman Park, 2 miles east of Downtown
Great wine selection and food. Spanish tapas and large plates: crispy cabbage, grilled hangar steak, chorizo with sweet & sour figs. Beautiful patio seating. Watering hole for many celebrities, Walking Dead, Vampire Diaries, to name a few.

BONES
3130 Piedmont Rd. NE, 404-237-2663
www.bonesrestaurant.com
CUISINE: Steakhouse
DRINKS: Full Bar
SERVING: Lunch, Dinner
PRICE RANGE: $$$$
NEIGHBORHOOD: Buckhead
Recognized as the best steakhouse in Atlanta (don't

tell Kevin Rathbun), serving prime beef, fresh seafood, and Maine lobster along with Southern regional specialties. Great service.

BREAD & BUTTERFLY
290 Elizabeth St, 678-515-4536
www.bread-and-butterfly.com
CUISINE: French Cafe
DRINKS: Full Bar
SERVING: Breakfast, Lunch, Dinner
PRICE RANGE: $$
NEIGHBORHOOD:
Café/bistro serving seasonal, French-inspired cuisine. Inviting dark tufted banquette, café seating outside, comfortable stools at the bar, ferns hanging overhead. Favorites: Spiced Octopus and Truffled Penne Au Gratin. Shrimp remoulade that might remind you of the Commander's Palace in New Orleans. Decadent

desserts. Weekend brunch favorite. Reservations needed for groups of six or more.

BRICK STORE PUB
125 E Court Square, Decatur, 404-687-0990
www.brickstorepub.com
CUISINE: American
DRINKS: Full Bar
SERVING: Lunch & Dinner
PRICE RANGE: $$
NEIGHBORHOOD: Decatur
Casual eatery with a menu of pub grub and great selection of beers. Menu favorites include: Cast iron pot pie and Fish 'n' chips.

BRUSH SUSHI IZAKAYA
316 Church St, Decatur, 678-949-9412
www.brushatl.com
CUISINE: American (New), Diners
DRINKS: No Booze
SERVING: Dinner, Brunch on Sundays, Closed on Mondays
PRICE RANGE: $$
NEIGHBORHOOD: Decatur
High-end eatery offers a menu of Japanese small plates and sushi. Favorites: Chirashi and Wagyu Gyoza. Reservations recommended. Sit next to the sushi bar to watch the chefs in action.

BUSY BEE CAFÉ
810 Martin Luther King Jr Dr SW, 404-525-9212
www.thebusybeecafe.com
CUISINE: Soul Food

DRINKS: No Booze
SERVING: Lunch
PRICE RANGE: $$
NEIGHBOROOD: West End/Atlanta University
This old-school soul food eatery, around since 1947, is popular among locals and celebrities like Jay-Z. Here you'll find good home cooking serving favorites like collards, fried chicken and mac and cheese. Neck bones, anyone?

CAFÉ INTERMEZZO
1065 Peachtree Rd. NE, 470-878-3137
www.cafeintermezzo.com
CUISINE: Coffee & Tea, Desserts
DRINKS: Full Bar
SERVING: Lunch, Dinner
PRICE RANGE: $$
NEIGHBORHOOD: Midtown
They want you to think of this as a "European coffeehouse," but it's really just a big old tourist trap. "A visit is like stepping back over 100 years in Vienna." Well, no it's not. Gigantic 50-page menu has everything you can imagine and over 100 pastries. Impressive wine, Champagne and beer selection.

CANTON HOUSE
4825 Buford Hwy NE, Chamblee, 770-936-9030
www.cantonhouserestaurant.com
CUISINE: Dim Sum
DRINKS: Beer & Wine
SERVING: Lunch & Dinner
PRICE RANGE: $$

NEIGHBORHOOD: Chamblee
Casual eatery featuring a menu of dim sum and traditional Cantonese cuisine. Menu favorites include: Pork dumplings; Chicken feet; shrimp wrapped in fried tofu skin; rice noodle rolls stuffed with shrimp; radish cakes; Chinese sausage wrapped in lotus leaf.

CHAI PANI
406 W. Ponce de Leon Ave, Atlanta, 404-378-4030
www.chaipanidecatur.com
CUISINE: Indian
DRINKS: Full Bar
SERVING: Lunch & Dinner
PRICE RANGE: $$
NEIGHBORHOOD: Decatur
Cute little café serving Indian "street food" and traditional Indian cuisine. Menu favorites include: Samosa smothered in tamarind and mint chutney. Vegan and gluten-free options available.

CHOPS LOBSTER BAR
70 W. Paces Ferry Rd. NW, 404-262-2675
www.buckheadrestaurants.com/
CUISINE: American; steakhouse
DRINKS: Full Bar
SERVING: dinner
PRICE RANGE: $$$
NEIGHBORHOOD: Buckhead
Steak tartare, bone-in ribeye, double Porterhouse, Kurobuta pork chop. Next to the St. Regis.

CHROME YELLOW TRADING CO.

501 Edgewood Ave SE, 470-355-1340
www.chromeyellowtradingco.com
CUISINE: Coffee & Tea
DRINKS: No Booze
SERVING: Breakfast, Lunch, Dinner
PRICE RANGE: $$
NEIGHBORHOOD: Old Fourth Ward
Unique mixture of a coffeeshop up in the front and retail shop offering trendy men's & women's fashions as well as ceramics. Coffee shop offers variety of coffees, teas, and pastries. Dog-friendly patio. The coffee beans come from Stumptown.

COLONNADE

1879 Cheshire Bridge Rd. NE, 404-874-465
www.thecolonnadeatlanta.com
CUISINE: American, Southern
DRINKS: Full Bar
SERVING: lunch / dinner
PRICE RANGE: $$
NEIGHBORHOOD: Morningside/Lenox Park
A popular family restaurant that is always filled with locals. Southern cooking at its finest, serving typical favorites like fried chicken, collard greens and mac-n-cheese. Giant portions. Excellent prime rib. Delicious desserts like strawberry shortcake with ice cream.

DESTA ETHIOPIAN KITCHEN

3086 Briarcliff Rd NE, 404-929-0011
www.destaethiopiankitchen.com
CUISINE: Ethiopian, Desserts, Sandwiches
DRINKS: Beer & Wine

SERVING: Lunch, Dinner
PRICE RANGE: $$
NEIGHBORHOOD: Briarcliff & 2nd location in
Emory Point
Locals favorite offering a variety of exotic dishes
with lots of seating under a roof outside. Vegetarian
options available. Favorites: Chicken and Ribeye
chunks and Fresh Grouper. The Tibs allows you to
"build your own meal," choosing your meat, carb and
a side. If you like spicy foods, this place is for you.

EL RAY DEL TACO
Pinetree West Shopping Center, 5288 Buford Hwy
NE, Doraville, 770-986-0032
www.elreydeltacoatl.com
CUISINE: Mexican
DRINKS: Beer & Wine
SERVING: Lunch & Dinner (open late)
PRICE RANGE: $

NEIGHBORHOOD: Doraville
A favorite late-night haunt known for its excellent
Mexican platters and tacos. You can watch them in
the kitchen making the corn tortillas to order. Menu
favorites include: Lengua (tongue) and carnita tacos.

EATS
600 Ponce De Leon Ave. NE, 404-888-9149
www.eatsonponce.net
CUISINE: Southern, Italian, Caribbean
DRINKS: Beer & Wine
SERVING: Lunch, Dinner
PRICE RANGE: $
NEIGHBORHOOD: Old Fourth Ward
An Atlanta mainstay offering a menu of healthy foods
and homestyle staples like jerk and BBQ chicken,
fettucini Alfredo and fresh vegetarian dishes.

EMPIRE STATE SOUTH
999 Peachtree St. NE, 404-541-1105
www.empirestatesouth.com
CUISINE: Southern; New Southern
DRINKS: Full Bar
SERVING: Breakfast, Lunch, Dinner
PRICE RANGE: $$$
NEIGHBORHOOD: Midtown
A community restaurant serving authentic Southern dishes focusing on the foods of the region. Try the oyster po'boy. But they have lots of other things you won't see on menus in Atlanta, like crispy sweetbreads and lamb belly with braised cabbage. When was the last time you had chicken consommé, at your granny's house? Here it's served with meatballs, boiled peanuts and root veggies. Yum. Chef here is Hugh Acheson, a judge on "Top Chef." Extensive coffee bar.

FARM BURGER
3365 Piedmont Rd. NE, 404-816-0603
www.farmburger.net
CUISINE: Burgers
DRINKS: Beer & Wine
SERVING: Lunch, Dinner
PRICE RANGE: $$
NEIGHBORHOOD: Buckhead
As the name implies, here it's all about the burgers, which are made from 100% fresh grass-fed beef. The menu is seasonal and sourced from local farms. You must try the Spicy Garlic and Parmesan Fries.

FAT MATT'S RIB SHACK

1811 Piedmont Ave NE, 404-607-1622
www.fatmattsribshack.com
CUISINE: Barbeque
DRINKS: Beer & Wine
SERVING: Lunch, Dinner
PRICE RANGE: $$
NEIGHBOROOD: Morningside/Lenox Park
It's a hole-in-the-wall but worth a visit. The food is
good, cheap and messy. Great ribs. Live Blues Music.

FELLINI'S PIZZA

4429 Roswell Rd. NE, 404-303-8248
www.fellinisatlanta.com
CUISINE: Pizza
DRINKS: Beer & Wine
SERVING: Lunch, Dinner
PRICE RANGE: $
NEIGHBORHOOD: several locations in Atlanta
Better than average pizza, ordered by the slice or pie.
Their white pizza is the best.

FLIP BURGER BOUTIQUE

1587 Howell Mill Rd. NW, 404-343-1609 – West
Midtown
www.flipburgerboutique.com
CUISINE: Burgers, American (New), Wine Bars
DRINKS: Full Bar
SERVING: Lunch, Dinner
PRICE RANGE: $$
NEIGHBORHOOD: Buckhead – West Midtown
A modern burger boutique featuring a menu that
redefines what we've come to think a hamburger

should be. In a modern space, FLIP incorporates elements of fine dining with a creative, raw energy. While they serve classic all-American burgers, they also have some interesting twists: try the Bun Mi, seared pork sausage with pickled ginger and Asian-spiced cole slaw. Or try one of their liquid-nitrogen milkshakes. You'll love the whimsicality of the place: the designer has a pair of white banquettes upside down to make a "roof" over the banquette you're sitting in. Visually stunning and fun.

FOX BROS BAR-B-Q
1238 Dekalb Ave Ne, 404-577-4030
www.foxbrosbbq.com
CUISINE: Barbeque/American (Traditional)
DRINKS: Full Bar
SERVING: Lunch & Dinner
PRICE RANGE: $$
Informal eatery offering up a menu of slow-roasted ribs, pulled pork, and Southern sides. Picks: Beef brisket and Spare Ribs. Nice patio for dining. Try the Frito pie.

FRED'S MEAT & BREAD
99 Krog St NE, Atlanta, 404-688-3733
www.fredsmeatandbread.com/
CUISINE: Burgers/Sandwiches
DRINKS: No Booze
SERVING: Lunch & Dinner
PRICE RANGE: $$$
NEIGHBORHOOD: Old Fourth Ward
Small sandwich shop serves international specialties. What elevates the sandwiches here is that the chef

uses only the best ingredients, so everything's top-notch. Menu favorites include: Pimiento Cheese Club and homemade fries. Simple, unpretentious comfort food.

GATO
1660 McLendon Ave, 404-371-0889
www.gatoatl.com
CUISINE: Breakfast & Brunch
DRINKS: Full Bar
SERVING: Breakfast, Lunch, & Dinner on Fri, Sat, & Sun
PRICE RANGE: $
NEIGHBORHOOD: Candler Park
Funky Tex-Mex café featuring breakfast (served all day), lunchtime sandwiches and dinner. Favorites: Sweet Potato chocolate chip pancakes for breakfast and Chicharra En Salpicón (pork belly served three ways) for dinner. Creative cocktails with nice Tequila selection.

THE GENERAL MUIR
Emory Point, 1540 Avenue Pl B-230, Atlanta, 678-927-9131
www.thegeneralmuir.com
CUISINE: American/Delis
DRINKS: Full Bar
SERVING: Breakfast, Lunch & Dinner
PRICE RANGE: $$
NEIGHBORHOOD: Emory Point
Upscale New York-style Jewish deli (with some pleasant twists on old classics) with a menu that won't disappoint. More fun for breakfast and lunch

than later. Smoked salmon over latkes & sour cream; a skyscraper of a pastrami sandwich with lots of whole grain mustard; burgers with 2 patties, Russian dressing & American cheese; a delicious Rueben and Matzo Ball soup. Fridays only they serve their version of fried chicken—marinated overnight, then dredged in flour and corn starch before they steam it. That's right, it's steamed before they fry it. But wait'll you taste it. Some of the crunchiest skin you've ever had on fried chicken. But remember, Fridays only.

GUNSHOW
924 Garrett St, Atlanta, 404-380-1886
www.gunshowatl.com
CUISINE: Southern; New American
DRINKS: Full Bar
SERVING: Dinner Tues – Sat from 6 to 9
PRICE RANGE: $$$
NEIGHBORHOOD: Glenwood Park
This is rock star Chef Kevin Gillespie's take on a combination of Chinese dim sum and Brazilian churrascaria-style dining. I know of 2 or 3 places in the country where they have the guy who actually cooks the food bring it out to your table. In this way, you get to talk to the chef about the dish he's made. Here, they using rolling carts and trays and the chefs bring out what they've made for you to see. If you like it, you order it. It's a big open environment here, with communal style tables, a big open kitchen where you can see Kevin and his co-chefs working up a sweat. Menu changes daily, but it's always new and

interesting. Well worth a stop. (When you see the red-bearded Chef Kevin roaming around the room, don't be embarrassed to ask for a photo with him. You won't be the first.) Kevin has a great cookbook, also: "Pure Pork Awesomeness."

HEIRLOOM MARKET BBQ
2243 Akers Mill Rd SE, 770-612-2502
www.heirloommarketbbq.com
CUISINE: Barbeque
DRINKS: No Booze
SERVING: Lunch, Dinner
PRICE RANGE: $$
NEIGHBOROOD: Smyrna/Vinings
Food is amazing here. Delicious mouth-watering ribs, pulled chicken and mac 'n cheese with red chili. The guys here make their ribs in the Korean style, rubbing the ribs with "gochujang" (a hot-n-spicy paste). They are quick to tell you that Korean BBQ was being

made 3,000 years before American was founded.

(They have 5 varieties of sauces to try.) The catch is that because of a local ordinance this place is now take-out only, but you can eat standing up out on their patio in good weather.

HOMEGROWN
968 Memorial Dr. SE, 404-222-0455
www.homegrownga.com
CUISINE: Breakfast & Brunch, Vegetarian
DRINKS: No Alcohol
SERVING: Breakfast, Lunch
PRICE RANGE: $
NEIGHBORHOOD: East Atlanta
A "laid-back" coffee shop serving "top-notch" Southern food (breakfast all day) using fresh ingredients and locally grown produce.

JCT KITCHEN & BAR
1198 Howell Mill Rd., 404-355-2252
www.jctkitchen.com
CUISINE: Southern
DRINKS: Full Bar
SERVING: Lunch, Dinner, Brunch
PRICE RANGE: $$
NEIGHBORHOOD: West Midtown
Southern cooking at its best. Fried chicken, Shrimp & Grits and North Georgia Trout are just a few of the tasty menu selections. Live music Thurs. Fri. & Sat.

KEVIN RATHBUN STEAK HOUSE
154 Krog St. NE, 404-524-5600
www.kevinrathbunsteak.com
CUISINE: Steakhouse

DRINKS: Full Bar
SERVING: Dinner
PRICE RANGE: $$$$
NEIGHBORHOOD: Inman Park
In Inman Park, you'll find this top notch steakhouse with an excellent wine list. This guy beat Bobby Flay on "Iron Chef America." Here you'll see why: eggplant fries, Coca-cola baby back ribs with a cabbage-scallion slaw that's really tasty, a Maine lobster tail (half or whole) served cold as a starter, dry aged cowboy ribeye (22 oz), ribeye (10 or 20 oz), filets, strips, chops. Great sides, as you'd expect: braised greens with hog jowl, twice-baked potato, Parmesan fries. One of four of Kevin Rathbun's Atlanta restaurants. All are worth visiting.

KIMBALL HOUSE
303 E Howard Ave, Decatur, 404-378-3502
www.kimball-house.com
CUISINE: New Southern
DRINKS: Full Bar
SERVING: Dinner
PRICE RANGE: $$$
NEIGHBORHOOD: Decatur
The bar here is really fun, as it's set in Decatur's old train station. High ceilings, tall windows that let in lots of light. The bar specializes in absinthe-based cocktails. An oyster lovers' haven, Kimball House offers as many varieties of the bivalve as the Oyster Bar in Grand Central Station. (Or so it seems.) Menu favorites include: Lobster & Artichoke tarte and Chicken Roulade, but since the menu changes daily, you're never sure. What you can be sure of, however,

is the consistent high quality of the food here. Take the butter beans, a staple in many Southern diets. The French-trained chefs here glaze them with butter, lemon and garlic. The teeny bits of house-cured ham set this dish apart. You could eat a big bowl of them. If you have time for only one thing to do in Decatur, this would be my choice.

KING + DUKE
3060 Peachtree Rd, Atlanta, 404-477-3500
www.kinganddukeatl.com
CUISINE: American
DRINKS: Full Bar
SERVING: Lunch & Dinner
PRICE RANGE: $$$
NEIGHBORHOOD: Buckhead
Another restaurant from Chef Ford Fry, this eatery offers a seasonal dining experience. A 24-foot open hearth is the main focus of this restaurant as many of the dishes are cooked over wood. Menu favorites include: Yorkshire pudding, aged, bone-in rib eye and

Mississippi rabbit with liver toast. Menu changes
often.

LA FONDA LATINA
2813 Peachtree Rd. NE, 404-816-8311
www.lafondaatlanta.com
CUISINE: Cuban
DRINKS: Full Bar
SERVING: Lunch, Dinner
PRICE RANGE: $
NEIGHBORHOOD: several locations in Atlanta
Good solid Cuban food with dishes like the Cuban
Sandwich platter that comes with black beans and
rice. (I'm from Miami, so I know good Cuban food.
This is *v-e-r-y* close.)

La Grotta Ristorante Italiano

LA GROTTA
2637 Peachtree Rd. NE, 404-231-1368
www.lagrottaatlanta.com
CUISINE: Italian

DRINKS: Full Bar
SERVING: Dinner
PRICE RANGE: $$$
NEIGHBORHOOD: Midtown
An Atlanta tradition since 1978, this eatery offers delicious fare in a beautiful atmosphere with great service. Voted Best Italian Restaurant for many years by *Atlanta Magazine*.

LA OAXAQUENA TAQUERIA
605 Mt Zion Rd, Jonesboro, 770-960-3010
www.taquerialaoaxaquena.com
CUISINE: Mexican
DRINKS: No Booze
SERVING: Lunch, Dinner
PRICE RANGE: $$
Casual Mexican eatery featuring tacos & Oaxacan specialties. Salsa bar. Favorites: Tortas Tlayudas (an authentic Oazacan delicacy).

LADYBIRD GROVE & MESS HALL
684 John Wesley Dobbs Ave NE, Atlanta, 404-458-6838
http://www.ladybirdatlanta.com/
CUISINE: American (New)
DRINKS: Full Bar
SERVING: Lunch & Dinner
PRICE RANGE: $$
NEIGHBORHOOD: Old Fourth Ward
A hip rustic themed restaurant and bar with a menu of New American cuisine. Menu favorites include: Spatchcock Chicken and the Double decker burger. Don't leave without trying the Navajo Fry Bread.

This dish starts out as a piece of bread that's fried until crispy. Then it's covered with Benton's country ham sliced thinly and topped with cilantro and some black pepper. Then, to provide contrast, honey is dribbled over the whole thing.

LANZHOU RAMEN
5231 Buford Hwy NE, Doraville, 678-691-2175
www.lanzhouramenatlanta.com
CUISINE: Chinese, Ramen
DRINKS: No Booze
SERVING: Lunch, Dinner
PRICE RANGE: $
The mainstay is the hand-pulled noodles (LanZhou is named after a type of hand-pulled noodle). There's even a noodle viewing window in the back. Over 30 noodle dishes on the menu. Nice large portions. Favorites: Xiao long bao (Shanghai soup buns) and Pork Meatball soup.

LEON'S FULL SERVICE
131 E Ponce De Leon Ave., Decatur, 404-687-0500
www.leonsfullservice.com
CUISINE: Gastropubs, American (Traditional)
DRINKS: Full Bar
SERVING: Lunch, Dinner
PRICE RANGE: $$
NEIGHBORHOOD: Decatur
The name says it all. At Full Service you get it all: great food and great service. Known for their specialty cocktails. Try the One-Eyed Jack: rye, root, maple and bitters. Superior beer list, including over a dozen on draft. (Try the local beer, Red Brick Porter.)

worth going to Decatur. Menu selections include: chicken sausage, chickpea salad, veggie loaf and molasses toffee pudding.

LITTLE TART BAKESHOP
99 Krog St, 404-348-4797
www.littletartatl.com/
CUISINE: Coffee shop; pastries; light fare
DRINKS: Beer & wine
SERVING: Breakfast, Lunch, Dinner
PRICE RANGE: $$
NEIGHBORHOOD: Grant Park
Discovered this (as well as the **Octane** coffee shop) after visiting the Oakland Cemetery just a few feet away. Then I remembered Anthony Bourdain mentioning the place in one of his shows. Ham and cheese croissant is the best. Among the sweet treats: their superior pecan pie and the strawberry galette.

MASTERPIECE
3940 Buford Hwy, Duluth, 770-622-1191
www.masterpiece-chinese.com
CUISINE: Szechuan
DRINKS: No Booze
SERVING: Lunch, Dinner, Closed Tuesdays
PRICE RANGE: $$
NEIGHBORHOOD: Duluth
Chinese eatery serving authentic Chinese cuisine with a focus on Szechuan, Cantonese and Hunan style. Nothing charming or quaint about this place, but really good quality cuisine. Most dishes are hot, hot, hot, so be careful when you order. Favorites: Pork

Belly, Pork with hot Peppers, Tea-smoked Duck, and Pork Soup Dumplings.

MEDITERRANEA RESTAURANT & BAKERY
332 Ormond St SE, 404-748-4219
www.mediterraneaatl.com
CUISINE: Mediterranean, Bakery
DRINKS: Full Bar
SERVING: Breakfast, Lunch, Dinner, Brunch,
Closed Mon & Tues
PRICE RANGE: $$
NEIGHBORHOOD: Grant Park
Located in an historic building, this chic place offers a creative menu of gluten-free and Mediterranean fare. Popular brunch spot, especially the upper outdoor level where in good weather you can lunch or dine under a canopy of trees. Favorites: Calabrese Shrimp with Orzo, Orange marmalade Cream cheese French toast and Chicken sausage with gravy. Even the pastries are gluten-free.

MILLER UNION
999 Brady Ave., 678-733-8550
www.millerunion.com/
CUISINE: New Southern / American
DRINKS: Full bar
SERVING: Lunch, Dinner
PRICE RANGE: $$$
NEIGHBORHOOD: West Midtown
Chef Steven Satterfield (James Beard Award for Best Chef Southeast in 2017) bases his menu on ingredients available from week-to-week. Always a great experience if you're looking for the "new" in

Southern cuisine. Cornmeal breaded fried oysters, braised pork cheeks, homemade pork and sage sausage, grilled Vidalia onions.

MINERO
Ponce City Market
675 Ponce De Leon Ave, N.E., Atlanta, 404-532-1580
www.minerorestaurant.com
CUISINE: Mexican
DRINKS: TBA
SERVING: TBA
PRICE RANGE: $$
NEIGHBORHOOD: Old Fourth Ward
Chef Sean Brock, famed for his Husk restaurants in Charleston and Nashville, is opening this Southern-Mexican spot. Expect things like tacos made with catfish and burritos with hoppin' John. Yes!

NO. 246
129 E Ponce De Leon Ave., Decatur, 678-399-8246
www.no246.com
CUISINE: Italian; New Southern
DRINKS: Full Bar
SERVING: Lunch, Dinner
PRICE RANGE: $$
NEIGHBORHOOD: Decatur
Here Chef Ford Fry (who also owns **JCT Kitchen and Bar**) has a restaurant that serves Italian-inspired cuisine composed of local, farm fresh ingredients. What he really does is fuse Italian with Southern cooking to create a new kind of cuisine you won't

find anywhere else. Really. Try the broccoli soup with crispy pancetta and cheddar to start.

NORTHERN CHINA EATERY
5141 Buford Hwy NE, Atlanta, 770-458-2282
www.northernchinaeatery.com/
CUISINE: Chinese
DRINKS: No Booze
SERVING: Lunch & Dinner; closed Tues
PRICE RANGE: $
NEIGHBORHOOD: Doraville
Small put popular eatery. Lots of lamb dishes, and I especially like the cumin-rubbed skewers when they're the daily special. Menu favorites: Mandarin Pie (a pork dish) and Boiled cabbage with egg yolks; potato and carrot stir fry.

F
OLD BRICK PIT BARBEQUE
4805 Peachtree Rd, Chamblee, 770-986-7727
www.oldbrickpitbbq.com/

CUISINE: Barbeque
DRINKS: No Booze
SERVING: Lunch & Dinner; closed Sun
PRICE RANGE: $
NEIGHBORHOOD: Fairmont
Open since 1976, this place is known for their sauce made from a family recipe. Simple menu featuring items like pulled pork and ribs cooked in their hickory fired pit, Brunswick stew and peach cobbler. The dressing on the chopped pork has a spicy tomato tang to it you won't soon forget. Make sure you get a side of the lovely sweet cole slaw.

THE OPTIMIST
914 Howell Mill Rd., 404-477-6260
www.theoptimistrestaurant.com
CUISINE: Seafood; Southern
DRINKS: full bar
SERVING: Lunch, Dinner
PRICE RANGE: $$$

NEIGHBORHOOD: West Midtown
"Esquire" called this the best new restaurant in America in 2012 ("Bon Appétit" did the same thing in 2013) and it's easy to see why. The splendor is the room—a cavernous white ceiling supported by exposed steel trusses is most dramatic. There's an oyster bar with the contours of a surfboard (serving over 20 varieties). My feeling is that Chef Ford Fry owes a debt to some of the more edgy culinary trends emanating from nearby Charleston. This is why I recommend you try the she-crab soup with shrimp toast, followed by the octopus cooked Spanish style and served with watermelon before you dip your fork ever so gently into the red snapper in a lovely lime broth. Or the redfish in a cornmeal crust. If you're not in a seafood mood, get the bone-in pork chop. If you worship seafood, this is your temple. This place will remind you of the fish camps your parents took you to by the lake when you were a kid.

PARISH
240 N. Highland Ave., 404-681-4434
www.parishatl.com
CUISINE: Southern, American
DRINKS: Full Bar
SERVING: Breakfast, Lunch, Dinner
PRICE RANGE: $$
NEIGHBORHOOD: Inman Park
The reputation as one of Atlanta's top restaurants is well deserved. Serving delicious fresh food with live music. Pan fried catfish, steak tartare, country ham and chicken liver paté. The buttermilk fried chicken comes with collard greens and corn bread.

PHO DAI LOL #2
4186 Buford Hwy NE Ste G, Atlanta, 404-633-2111
No Website
CUISINE: Vietnamese
DRINKS: No Booze
SERVING: Lunch & Dinner
PRICE RANGE: $
NEIGHBORHOOD: Druid Hills
Located in a little plaza, the food sets this Vietnamese
eatery apart from the others. Menu features a variety
of Pho dishes and noodles. You can customize your
bowl with its rich beefy broth by adding cilantro,
mint, chili sauce, eye-round steak, brisket. The
possibilities are endless.

THE PIG & THE PEARL
1380 Atlantic Dr NW, Atlanta, 404-541-0930
www.thepigandthepearl.com/
CUISINE: Barbeque
DRINKS: Full Bar
SERVING: Lunch & Dinner
PRICE RANGE: $$
NEIGHBORHOOD: Atlantic Station
This family friendly eatery with a sleek modern look
offers a simple menu of smokehouse fare along with
oysters and crafted cocktails. Raw bar. The chef likes
the word "smokehouse" over "BBQ" because he adds
a bit of smoke to lots of different things, like chicken,
beef brisket with hickory and pecan woods. As an
appetizer, I'd recommend the lobster salad with
tarragon. Patio seating available when temperatures
allow.

POLARIS
265 Peachtree St NE, Atlanta, 404-460-6425
www.polarisatlanta.com
CUISINE: American
DRINKS: Full Bar
SERVING: Lunch & Dinner; closed Sun & Mon
PRICE RANGE: $$
NEIGHBORHOOD: Downtown
Located 22 stories atop the historic **Hyatt Regency Atlanta** hotel, this iconic rotating restaurant has been popular among tourists since the flying saucer-shaped revolving bar opened in 1967. It had gotten quite shabby and was closed in 2004 for a 10-year-long renovation job. Now even locals pop up for a drink and a look at the stunning view. I remember my first time up here. I didn't think there was anything to "see" in Atlanta. But I turned out to be wrong. Menu offers chef-inspired shared plates and handcrafted cocktails.

PORCH LIGHT LATIN KITCHEN
300 Village Green Cir SE, Smyrna, 678-309-9858
www.porchlightlatinkitchen.com
CUISINE: Latin American
DRINKS: Wine & Beer
SERVING: Lunch – Thurs, Fri & Sat, Dinner daily, Closed on Sunday
PRICE RANGE: $$
NEIGHBORHOOD: Smyrna
Latin American eatery offers a varied menu and creative cocktails. Simple but attractive decor with comfortable seating at the counter and a row of tables

against the wall. Narrow and cozy. Favorites: Puerto Rican Fried Pork Chop (something that needs to be seen as well as eaten, it's so wonderful, because it includes the loin chop with ribs, belly and skin) and Crispy braised beef citrus mojo. Delicious desserts like Tres Leches Cake. Book a table on the weekend.

THE PORTER BEER BAR
1156 Euclid Ave. NE, 404-223-0393
www.theporterbeerbar.com
CUISINE: American (New), Pubs
DRINKS: Beer & Wine
SERVING: Lunch, Dinner & Brunch
PRICE RANGE: $$
NEIGHBORHOOD: Little Five Points
A new restaurant serving American cuisine with a menu of small plates and sandwiches. The beer bar features a menu of over 800 beers.

PURE TAQUERIA

300 N Highland Ave. NE, 404-522-7873
www.puretaqueria.com
CUISINE: Mexican, Sandwiches, Tex-Mex
DRINKS: Full Bar
SERVING: Lunch & Dinner
PRICE RANGE: $$
NEIGHBORHOOD: Inman Park
A new take on an authentic Mexican taqueria.
Sophisticated and fun with tasty margaritas. Five
locations in Atlanta.

QUOC HUONG BANH MI FAST FOOD

5150 Buford Hwy NE, Atlanta, 770-936-0605
https://banhmiquochuong.com/
CUISINE: Vietnamese
DRINKS: No Booze
SERVING: Lunch & Dinner; closed Thurs.

PRICE RANGE: $$$
NEIGHBORHOOD: Doraville
Popular eatery offering a menu of Vietnamese banh mi sandwiches and pho noodle soups. They are actually better known for their sandwiches with their extra crispy rice-flour baguettes. The most-ordered item here is the sandwich stuffed with crunchy BBQed pork that has a spicy kick. The sandwiches are even better when you add a fried egg. Delicious smoothies and bubble tea.

R. THOMAS' DELUXE GRILL
1812 Peachtree St NW, 404-881-0246
www.rthomasdeluxegrill.net
CUISINE: Vegan, American (Traditional),
DRINKS: Beer & Wine
SERVING: Breakfast, Lunch, Dinner, Brunch
PRICE RANGE: $$
NEIGHBORHOOD: Buckhead
Outdoor eatery (has indoor seating as well) open 24/7 catering to both meat lovers and vegetarians. Great spot for breakfast (or any other meal) and you won't leave hungry. Favorites: any Breakfast dish, Smashed Potatoes with Mushroom Gravy, Cinnamon Sweet Potatoes, Ginger ahi tuna and Thai Express Bowl. Huge menu and all of it good. Don't overlook at superior side dishes. Nice selection of smoothies.

RATHBUN'S

112 Krog St. NE, 404-524-5600
www.rathbunsrestaurant.com/
CUISINE: New American
DRINKS: Full Bar
SERVING: Dinner
PRICE RANGE: $$$
NEIGHBORHOOD: Inman Park

This is Rathbun's flagship eatery with his upmarket take on some Southern classics in an industrial décor that's very slick. He has quite the mini-empire along Krog Street, and it's well deserved. Crispy duck breast, Thai risotto, flash-fried oysters (luscious), roasted bone marrow, elk chop, BBQ chicken with molasses and pepper—these are the standout dishes. Also here is **Krog Bar** (www.krogbar.com/), which has a great selection of small plates with lots of cheeses, charcuterie items, olives and little sandwiches on great bread.

RISING ROLL GOURMET
1180 W Peachtree St NW, Atlanta, 404-815-6787
www.risingroll.com
CUISINE: Deli/Sandwiches
DRINKS: No Booze
SERVING: Breakfast, Lunch
PRICE RANGE: $$
NEIGHBORHOOD: Downtown / Midtown, **several other locations**
This, perhaps the best deli in town, offers a menu of sandwiches, paninis, soups, salads and desserts. Portions are large and the specials are worth noting. Menu favorites include: Grilled chicken portabello panini and Mexicano chicken Panini.

RISING SON
124 N Avondale Rd, Avondale Estates, 404-600-5297
www.risingsonavondale.com
CUISINE: American (New), Diner food
DRINKS: Full Bar
SERVING: **Special Note on hours:** Breakfast & Lunch (Tues-Fri- 8-3); Brunch (Sat-Sun, 8-3); Dinner (Fri & Sat only, 5-9).
PRICE RANGE: $$
NEIGHBORHOOD: Avondale Estates
Locals who know their food know about this place— it serves Southern breakfast and lunch classics, but with a lot of fresh twists. Favorites: Crispy Breakfast Dumplings (ground pork, ginger, cilantro—this is really yummy), Fried chicken, Cheddar, Bacon on a Biscuit; Catfish & Grits. Artisan cocktails and beers with small wine list. Since they only service dinner Fri and Sat, the menu is always different, but if you're

in town one of those days, you'll find it worth your while to get a table here. There's nothing ordinary about this place.

SAGE WOODFIRE TAVERN
4505 Ashford Dunwoody, 770 804 8880
www.sagewoodfiretavern.com/
CUISINE: American
DRINKS: Full Bar
SERVING: Lunch weekdays; dinner from 5 (except Sunday, when it's closed)
PRICE RANGE: $$
NEIGHBORHOOD: North Perimeter Area
Fine dining, great elegant atmosphere. Shrimp bisque, a super meatloaf made with veal, beef and pork.

SERPAS
659 Auburn Ave. NE, 404-688-0040
www.serpasrestaurant.com
CUISINE: American (New); Creole, Southwestern, Asian fusion
DRINKS: Full Bar
SERVING: Lunch, Dinner, Brunch
PRICE RANGE: $$
NEIGHBORHOOD: Old Fourth Ward
Hip restaurant serving up New American fare with a Cajun inflection. Pigs in a blanket with homemade Andouille, flounder with gnocchi, duck confit. You'll love this massive dining room with its exposed pipes and hip industrial look.

SNACKBOXE BISTRO
6035 Peachtree Rd, Doraville, 770-417-8082

www.snackboxebistro.com
CUISINE: Laotian, Asian Fusion
DRINKS: Beer & Wine
SERVING: Lunch, Dinner
PRICE RANGE: $$
NEIGHBORHOOD: Doraville
Casual eatery with hard-on-the-butt metal chairs and plain wood tables serving street food with Laotian influence. Very tasty dishes. Favorites: Coconut Crispy Rice Dish and Nam Khao (with pork), Mok Pha (steamed fish). Reservations recommended.

SO BA VIETNAMESE
560 Gresham Ave SE, Atlanta, 404-627-9911
www.soba-eav.com
CUISINE: Vietnamese
DRINKS: Full Bar
SERVING: Dinner nightly, Lunch weekends
PRICE RANGE: $$$
NEIGHBORHOOD: East Atlanta Village
Typical Vietnamese eatery with a menu of classic Viet fare including pho, rice vermicelli and broken-rice dishes.

SOUTH CITY KITCHEN
1144 Crescent Ave. NE, 404-873-7358
www.southcitykitchen.com
CUISINE: Southern
DRINKS: Full Bar
SERVING: Lunch & Dinner
PRICE RANGE: $$$
NEIGHBORHOOD: Midtown
Serving fresh and contemporary new Southern cuisine
for 19 years. One of Atlanta's favorite restaurants.
Great dishes like: shrimp and grits, buttermilk fried
chicken, she-crab soup, fried green tomatoes and
banana pudding.

SOUTHERN ART & BOURBON BAR
Intercontinental
3315 Peachtree Rd. NE, 404-946-9070
www.southernart.com
CUISINE: American; New Southern
DRINKS: Full Bar
SERVING: Breakfast, Lunch, Dinner
PRICE RANGE: $$$
NEIGHBORHOOD: Buckhead
Located in the Intercontinental, Chef Art Smith offers
a menu of Southern comforts and traditional classics.
Try the Buttermilk fried chicken, which comes squash
casserole, garlic green beans and red pepper gravy.
There's also a "Ham Bar" offering a variety of pork

products. If there's room, check out the vintage dessert table. Bar and lounge area.

SOUTHERN SOUL BARBEQUE
2020 Demere Rd, Saint Simons Island, 912-638-7685
www.southernsoulbbq.com/
CUISINE: Barbeque/Soul Food
DRINKS: Beer & Wine Only
SERVING: Lunch & Dinner
PRICE RANGE: $$
NEIGHBORHOOD: Saint Simons Island
Located in a former gas station, this Southern BBQ joint serves favorites like oak-smoked meat, BBQ turkey, pork shoulder and brisket.

SPRING
36 Mill St, Marietta, 678-540-2777
www.springmarietta.com
CUISINE: American (New)
DRINKS: Beer & Wine
SERVING: Dinner, Closed Sun & Mon
PRICE RANGE: $$$
NEIGHBORHOOD: Marietta
Located in the historic Marietta Square, this small eatery (with simple bare wooden tables, wooden floor, rustic brick walls) offers a creative seasonal menu (very limited but excellent selection) featuring locally sourced foods. It's won numerous awards, and is a destination for local foodies who insist on the highest quality and know they'll get it here.
Favorites: Tuna Crudo (with basil, cucumber, fennel), Halibut (pan roasted with zucchini, onions, wax beans, tomato, dill, butter), and my favorite, Quail

pan-roasted with rice grits, andouille, chanterelle and corn. You likely won't have these items to choose from because the menu changes abruptly. One good thing about this is that if you're local, you'll keep coming back to see what great things the inventive chef has done to treat Southern food with French cooking techniques. Extensive wine list.

ST CECILIA
3455 Peachtree Rd, Atlanta, 404-554-9995
www.stceciliaatl.com
CUISINE: Seafood/Italian
DRINKS: Full Bar
SERVING: Lunch weekdays, Dinner nightly
PRICE RANGE: $$$
NEIGHBORHOOD: Buckhead
A friendly upscale eatery with a menu of Italian seafood and pasta offered in a glamorous venue with high ceilings soaring up 3 floors. Reclaimed woods in shades of color you never thought existed is used on the walls in a very dramatic space with white tiled columns. The 20-seat marble bar is my favorite place to hang out, of course. Not much of a Southern slant to the food, which leans more toward Asia and Europe for the menu's inspiration, which is fine with me. Menu favorites include: Rabbit pasta, smoky octopus with Italian bean salad & oregano, cobia crudo with trout roe. Impressive wine selection.

STAPLEHOUSE
541 Edgewood Ave SE, 404524-5005
www.staplehouse.com
CUISINE: American (New)

DRINKS: Full Bar
SERVING: Dinner, Brunch, closed Mon & Tues
PRICE RANGE: $$$
NEIGHBORHOOD: Old Fourth Ward
In this century-old brick building, you'll find the most unusual restaurant & and bar benefiting The Giving Kitchen charity offers a rotating seasonal menu. Herbs are grown on the patio. Chicken liver mousse is superior, beets served with house-cured bresaola are just perfect. Tables are reservations only with bar seats first come first served. Food is excellent if you're lucky enough to get a table. I always get there early and snatch a seat at the bar. (The Giving Kitchen provides funds for people in the restaurant industry who have medical bills. All the profits after payroll and taxes go to the charity.)

STORICO FRESCO ALIMENTARI E RISTORANTE
3167 Peachtree Rd NE, 404-500-2181
www.storicofresco.com
CUISINE: Italian, Cooking Classes
DRINKS: Full Bar
SERVING: Lunch, Dinner, Closed Sundays
PRICE RANGE: $$
NEIGHBORHOOD: Buckhead
A true Italian Alimentari e Ristorante focusing on traditional and nearly lost Italian dishes. It's a big open room with bright lighting. Tables in the middle of the room are surrounded by the deli market counter and a wall of coolers holding grocery items. This Italian grocery store and restaurant combination offer a true Italian experience. The food is fresh, authentic,

and already cooked for the most part. Favorites: Cacio e Pepe and Chitarra Arrabbiata. Leave room for the delicious home-made Italian desserts. Nice wine selection.

SUNDIAL
Peachtree Center / Westin Hotel
210 Peachtree St. NW, 404 589-7506
www.sundialrestaurant.com/
CUISINE: American
DRINKS: Full Bar
SERVING: lunch / dinner
PRICE RANGE: $$
NEIGHBORHOOD: Downtown
The Sundial is the famous restaurant atop the Westin. It's certainly not famous for its food, but for the full view of Atlanta you get while you dine as the restaurant rotates 360 degrees.

SUSHI HOUSE HAYAKAWA

5979 Buford Hwy NE A10, Atlanta, 770-986-0010
www.atlantasushibar.com/
CUISINE: Japanese/Sushi
DRINKS: Full Bar
SERVING: Dinner; closed Mon & Tues
PRICE RANGE: $$$
NEIGHBORHOOD: Doraville
Classic Japanese eatery with a creative menu of sushi
and hot dishes. (One of the top 2 or 3 sushi places in
Atlanta.) Menu favorites include: Eel roll and
Butabara (grilled pork belly on a skewer).

TED'S MONTANA GRILL

133 Luckie St. NW, 404-521-9796
www.tedsmontanagrill.com
CUISINE: Burgers, American (Traditional)
DRINKS: Full Bar
SERVING: Lunch & Dinner
PRICE RANGE: $$
NEIGHBORHOOD: Downtown (plus 2 other
locations in Midtown & Decatur)
Owned by Ted Turner (who often stops by for
dinner), here you'll enjoy traditional American fare as
well as treats like Buffalo burgers. All the burgers are
top-notch. Friendly service.

THANK U CHICKEN

3473 Old Norcross Rd, Duluth, 470-875-9000
www.thankuchicken.com
CUISINE: Korean/Chicken Wings
DRINKS: Wine & Beer Only
SERVING: Lunch & Dinner; Closed Tues

PRICE RANGE: $$

Cheap eatery that's a great pick for a quick bite. Sports bar with a half dozen big TVs. It's in a less-than-glamorous strip mall outside Atlanta in Duluth, but the food's spectacular. It's not your usual "Southern fried chicken" joint, because the owners are Korean. The breading is quite unique—created from a blend of grains, mostly rice, that results in a very crispy skin. The most popular choice here is the chicken platter, half of it prepared in this "Southern" style and the other half coated in a sweet chili sauce. Favorites: Boneless soy sauce chicken and Boneless chicken with waffles. Great specials.

TICONDEROGA CLUB
99 Krog St NE, 404-458-4534
www.ticonderogaclub.com
CUISINE: American (Traditional)/Cocktail bar
DRINKS: Full Bar
SERVING: Dinner, Brunch on Sunday, closed on Wed.
PRICE RANGE: $$
NEIGHBORHOOD: Inman Park

Cozy retro-inspired eatery in the Krog Street Market with a creative menu and tasty craft cocktails. Favorites: Dry aged roasted duck, Vietnamese shrimp skewers and Scallops with asparagus and celery root cream. Great selection of ciders and sherries. No reservations and it's often crowded.

TINY LOU'S
Hotel Clermont
789 Ponce De Leon Ave, 470-485-0085

www.tinylous.com
CUISINE: French, Brasseries
DRINKS: Full Bar
SERVING: Dinner, Brunch on Sat & Sun
PRICE RANGE: $$
NEIGHBORHOOD: Poncey / Highland
French favorites (with lots of Southern twists) served in the intimate atmosphere of the downstairs level of the very fun Hotel Clermont (there's also a nice bar in the lobby as well as a great rooftop when the weather's good, so check those out as well). Favorites: Vidalia Onion Soup, Black Cocoa Foie Gras Torchon, Blue Ridge Trout Almondine and Roasted Octopus Niçoise. French focused wine list with crafted cocktails. You must save room for dessert with selections like the decadent chocolate Royale made with Venezuelan chocolate mousse and served with coffee cream. Classic French desserts made daily.

TWISTED SOUL COOKHOUSE & POURS
Apex West Midtown
1133 Huff Rd NW, 404-350-5500
www.twistedsoulcookhouseandpours.com
CUISINE: Soul Food, Desserts, Southern
DRINKS: Full Bar
SERVING: Lunch, Dinner, Closed Mondays
PRICE RANGE: $$
NEIGHBORHOOD: Midtown
Casual eatery offering a modern take on traditional soul food. Interesting twists on classic Southern dishes where the chef attacks the traditional dish and gussies it up with rigorous fine dining techniques,

making almost everything better, in my not-so-humble opinion. Cleaner, less grease, more style. Comfortable seating at the bar or at tables in a medium-sized simply decorated dining room. Favorites: Marinated Fried Chicken dipped in pot liquor and Country Style Pork Ribs with Coca Cola Gochujang Sauce. Try to leave room for Ivy's Heavenly Peach Cobbler. Large parties should call ahead.

TWO URBAN LICKS
820 Ralph McGill Blvd NE, 404-522-4622
www.twourbanlicks.com
CUISINE: American
DRINKS: Full Bar
SERVING: Dinner only
PRICE RANGE: $$$
NEIGHBORHOOD: Old Fourth Ward & Poncey-Highlands area
Industrial chic décor. The "salmon chips" are a big favorite here, but the fish tacos are good too. Pork spring rolls, short ribs, Vidalia onion soup. Duck and lamb are winners, too. Wine is on tap which is unique and there's a huge selection. Amazing food, right off the Beltline which afford a superior view.

THE VARSITY
61 North Ave NW, 404-881-1706
www.thevarsity.com
CUISINE: Fast Food
DRINKS: No Booze
SERVING: Lunch, Dinner
PRICE RANGE: $

NEIGHBOROOD: Midtown
This is the World's Largest Drive-in, with 800 seats, stands on more than two acres. Nearly 30,000 people will visit The Varsity during a Georgia Tech football game. More than two miles of hot dogs, a ton of onion rings, and 5,000 homemade pies daily. The downtown location is the world's largest single outlet for Coca-Cola. The dogs here are served "naked," minus any toppings, or the best way: with chili, cheese & cole slaw, which is something of a tradition down South.

W. H. STILES FISH CAMP
Central Food Hall - Ponce City Market
675 Ponce de Leon Ave, Atlanta, 678-235-3929
http://www.starprovisions.com/whstilesfish-camp
CUISINE: Seafood
DRINKS: Beer & wine
SERVING: Brunch, Dinner
PRICE RANGE: $$$
NEIGHBORHOOD: Fairmont
A casual fish shack that is basically a sandwich shop but also serves creative salads and seafood. Menu favorites include: Shrimp boil, Steamed fish bowls, raw bar.

WRECKING BAR BREWPUB
292 Moreland Ave NE, 404-221-2600
www.wreckingbarbrewpub.com
CUISINE: American (New), Brewpub
DRINKS: Full Bar
SERVING: Dinner, Lunch on Fri, Sat, & Sun
PRICE RANGE: $$

NEIGHBORHOOD: Little Five Points
Located in the basement of an old Victorian mansion, this gastropub offers creative menu selections for each meal and an impressive list of brews. The brews come from a 7-barrel brewing system right next door, with selections ranging from porters to stouts to lagers. Favorites: Catfish filet and Beef heart tartare. A lot of the food comes from their own farm. Their burger is one of the best Atlanta has to offer.

YALLA!
99 Krog St NE, 404-506-9999
www.yallaatl.com
CUISINE: Middle Eastern/Greek
DRINKS: No Booze
SERVING: Lunch, Dinner
PRICE RANGE: $$
NEIGHBORHOOD: Inman Park
Cute Middle Eastern food stall located next to Fred's Meat & Bread. A sandwich will feed 2 and often 3 people. Offerings: pita, laffa, and alla. Favorites: Spit roasted chicken and Israeli salad. Also excellent is the roasted lamb sandwich served with pickled turnips and rutabaga. Melts in your mouth.

Chapter 5
NIGHTLIFE

DAD'S GARAGE
569 Ezzard St., SE Atlanta, 404 523 3141
www.dadsgarage.com
NEIGHBORHOOD: Little Five Points
Known as one of Atlanta's best venues for improv comedy, original plays and other events. The audience can even choose themes the comics have to work with.

CLERMONT LOUNGE
789 Ponce De Leon Ave. NE, 404-874-4783
www.clermontlounge.net
NEIGHBORHOOD: Downtown East
The Clermont is Atlanta's oldest strip club and consistently ranked as one of the coolest dive bars anywhere. It's been around since 1965 and they pride themselves on the fact you can bring your grandmother here. Maybe that's because some of the dancers are almost as old as grandma. One of the standout performers, Blondie, is famous for demolishing beer cans with her... well, you get the idea. Lots of fun. Cheap drinks, karaoke, and live music.

COMPOUND
1008 Brady Ave. NW, 404-898-1702
www.compoundatl.com
NEIGHBORHOOD: West Midtown
A dance club with great music (usually hip-hop).

CYPRESS STREET PINT & PLATE
817 West Peachtree St. NE, 404-815-9243
http://cypressatl.com
NEIGHBORHOOD: Midtown
A restaurant and bar with a neighborhood pub vibe. Great burgers and excellent selection of beers.

THE EARL
488 Flat Shoals Ave. SE, 404-522-3950
www.badearl.com
NEIGHBORHOOD: East Atlanta

This restaurant and lounge is known for its alternative music. Good music and good food.

GOLD ROOM
2416 Piedmont Rd. NE, 404 400-5062
www.goldroomatlanta.com
NEIGHBORHOOD: Lindbergh
Upscale multi-level lounge and dance club in Lindbergh Center that attracts a lively crowd.

HAVANA CLUB
3112 Piedmont Rd., 404-941-4847
www.havanaclubatl.com/
Web site down at press time
NEIGHBORHOOD: Buckhead
This big dance club has different rooms offering different styles of music. But it's all fun.

MJQ CONCOURSE
736 Ponce De Leon Ave. NE, 404-870-0575
www.mjqofficial.com
NEIGHBORHOOD: Virginia Highlands
A club with an "underground" atmosphere that attracts a young crowd. A two-room space located in an old parking garage with a main basement room with a dance floor and a lounge room. Music mostly old school hip-hop or '80s & '90s with occasional bookings of blues and jazz acts.

MONDAY NIGHT BREWING
670 Trabert Ave NW, Atlanta, 404-352-7703
www.mondaynightbrewing.com

NEIGHBORHOOD: Westside / Home Park
An Atlanta-based craft brewery that brews balanced, flavorful ales. It was opened by 3 guys who left the corporate world to launch this place in the industrial-chic Westside District. These guys used to meet every Monday night to home-brew some beer, and now this.

NORTHSIDE TAVERN
1058 Howell Mill Rd. NW, 404-874-8745
www.northsidetavern.com
NEIGHBORHOOD: West Midtown
Voted one of the Top Ten Dive Bars in America. Great watering hole with cheap drinks and great music. Hosts some of the best local and regional Blues & Jazz acts.

OCTOPUS BAR
560 Gresham Ave SE, Atlanta, 404-627-9911
www.octopusbaratl.com/
NEIGHBORHOOD: East Atlanta

A late-night favorite of hipsters is this pub with an unmarked door nestled behind a "pho" house in East Atlanta. This graffiti-covered bar offers an impressive menu of wine and champagne. Nice simple menu of snacks like salt & pepper shrimp and Korean pork. Closed Sunday.

THE PORTER BEER BAR
1156 Euclid Ave NE, 404-223-0393
www.theporterbeerbar.com
NEIGHBORHOOD: Little Five Points
Extensive menu of over 800 beers with excellent food as well. Offers a variety of special events from beer tastings and festivals, to classes and themed dinners.

PUNCHLINE COMEDY CLUB
3652 Roswell Rd, 404-252-5233
www.punchline.com
NEIGHBORHOOD: Sandy Springs
Been here since 1982. Over 3,000 comics have performed in this, the granddaddy of Atlanta comedy venues.

SUTRA LOUNGE
1136 Crescent Ave. NE, 404-914-2184
sutraloungeatl.com/
NEIGHBORHOOD: Midtown
Top 40, hip hop bar. Great place to meet, flirt and maybe get lucky.

THE TABERNACLE
152 Luckie St. NW, 404-659-9022
www.tabernacleatl.com

NEIGHBORHOOD: Downtown
This mid-sized concert hall has hosted notable acts like Guns N' Roses, The Black Crowes, Fergie and Adele, Lenny Kravitz, Counting Crows. In 1910,this building was a tabernacle. Intimate venue insures you get close to the artists.

TIKI TANGO
57 13th St. NE, 404-873-6189
www.tikitangoatl.com
NEIGHBORHOOD: Midtown
A mega-bar with 3 levels, 6 bars, VIP accommodations and some of the hottest DJs in the city. Four dance floors. World-class DJs spin the latest House, Top 40, '80s, Funk & Hip-Hop.

TONGUE AND GROOVE
565 Main St NE, 404-261-2325
www.tandgonline.com/
NEIGHBORHOOD: Buckhead
This popular dance club in the Lindbergh Center off Piedmont Road in Buckhead offers hip hop, R&B, good range of music in a very elegant, sleek setting. Good bartenders, right on top of things. Has 8,500 square feet of things going on. Very sharp place.

TWO URBAN LICKS
820 Ralph McGill Blvd. NE, 404-522-4622
www.twourbanlicks.com
NEIGHBORHOOD:
Known as the "club with food." A great night out with live music that includes great food. Free valet parking.

Chapter 6
GAY NIGHTLIFE

Midtown is arguably the heart of gay life in Atlanta, particularly centered around the corner of **10th** and **Piedmont/Juniper**.

BLAKE'S ON THE PARK
227 10th St. NE, 404-454-7715
www.blakesontheparkatlanta.com/
NEIGHBORHOOD: Midtown
Lots of great music here in this bustling place. They have 24 video monitors. Also has a pretty good wide-ranging menu with everything from good burgers, wraps, salads, Chicago style hot dog, sandwiches (French dip and grilled cheese) and egg dishes (my favorite is the Hangover sandwich: 2 fried eggs, sausage & American cheese on a toasted roll).

BULLDOG BAR
893 Peachtree St. NE, 404-872-3025
No web site at press time.
NEIGHBORHOOD: Midtown
Big black club here in Atlanta. Small dance floor, so if you can't bump up against someone, you're not really trying.

THE COCKPIT
465 Boulevard SE, 404-343-2450
www.thecockpit-atlanta.blogspot.com
NEIGHBORHOOD: Grant Park
A gay bar filled with good old-fashioned macho men, well maybe not old fashioned. You'll find hot mechanics, delivery men, truck drivers, construction workers, and firemen.

THE HERETIC
2069 Cheshire Bridge Rd. NE, 404-325-3061
www.hereticatlanta.com
NEIGHBORHOOD:
A gay dance bar with an edge. Here you'll find TV

screens showing nude male models and a leather shop in he back. Wednesday night is fetish night so you have to dress the part.

MARY'S
1287 Glenwood Ave., 404-624-4411
www.marysatlanta.com
NEIGHBORHOOD: East Atlanta
Consistently voted one of the best gay bars (and dance clubs) not only in Atlanta, but the whole country. Karaoke (over 15,000 songs), DJs, everything; it's all here. Full schedule.

MY SISTER'S ROOM
84 12 St. NE, 678-705-4585
www.mysistersroom.com
NEIGHBORHOOD: Grant Park
Best lesbian bar in Atlanta. Dance floor, good music.
$5 cover.

OSCAR'S
1510 Piedmont Ave. NE, 404-815-8841
www.oscarsatlanta.com/
NEIGHBORHOOD: Midtown at Ansley Square
This is a big gay "martini & video bar." Full weekly
schedule. Check web site for details.

SWINGING RICHARDS
1400 Northside Dr NW, 404-352-0532
www.swingingrichards.com
NEIGHBORHOOD: Westside/Home Park
This Atlanta institution serves up some of the hottest
male studs you've ever seen and they are all
wonderfully nude. No cover on Tuesday before
midnight. Sorry ladies but it's men only.

WOOFS
494 Plasters Ave NE, 404-869-9422
www.woofsatlanta.com
NEIGHBORHOOD: Midtown
Woofs is a gay sports bar. Lots of flatscreen TVs for
sports fans. Game nights. Decent bar food and
friendly crowd.

Chapter 7
WHAT TO SEE & DO

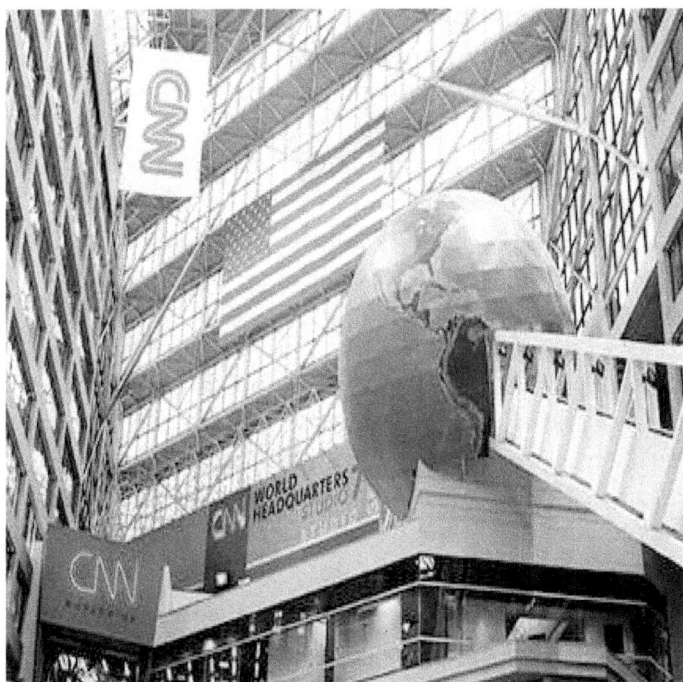

ATLANTA CITYPASS
www.citypass.com
Get one of these to save time and money on some of
the bigger attractions in town. Adults $74, kids $54.
The Georgia Aquarium
World of Coca-Cola

Inside CNN Atlanta Studio Tour
Zoo Atlanta or Atlanta History Center
Fernbank Museum of Natural History or High
Museum of Art

**APEX (AFRICAN-AMERICAN PANORAMIC
EXPERINCE) MUSEUM**
135 Auburn Ave, Atlanta, 404-523-2739
www.apexmuseum.org
NEIGHBORHOOD: Downtown
HOURS: Tues–Sat, 10 a.m. – 5 p.m.
ADMISSION: Moderate fee
APEX is a museum focusing on Auburn's history
through exhibits, replicas & workshops. Museum
features exhibitions, self-guided tours, and special
presentations. There's an exhibit with life-sized
reproductions that show you the condition slaves
endured, including one that replicates how they were
packed into slave ships for transport to the New
World. There's an exhibit that emphasize the
creations of black inventors. They range from the
engineer that invented the traffic light to how Michael
Jackson created some of the special effects used in his
shows. Permanent and traveling exhibitions. The
Trolley Theater features a replica of the old trolley
of Auburn Avenue and a multimedia history
presentation.

CENTER FOR PUPPETRY ARTS
1404 Spring St NW, Atlanta, 404-873-3391
https://puppet.org/
NEIGHBORHOOD: Midtown
HOURS: Open daily

ADMISSION: Tickets sold for performances
A unique cultural experience for both children and adults. Enjoy the wonder and art of puppetry. The center offers performances, workshops and a hands-on museum

CNN CENTER
www.cnn.com/tour/
190 Marietta St., NW Atlanta, 404-827-2300
NEIGHBORHOOD: Downtown
It's easy to buy tickets online. Or see **Atlanta CityPass**. The atrium at the entrance of the CNN Center offers a few gift shops on the lower level. A great spot for buying souvenirs that display Georgia and TBS network logo merchandise, including CNN, HLN and Cartoon Network characters at the CNN Store.

EBENEZER BAPTIST CHURCH
101 Jackson St NE, Atlanta, 404-688-7300
https://ebenezeratl.org/
NEIGHBORHOOD: Downtown
A designated national historic site. This is the original church where Marin Luther King, Jr., and his father preached. The Gothic Revival building reopened in 2011 after a major restoration effort that made it look like it did in the 1960s when the Kings worked here. (The microphones in the pulpit are the originals used back then.)

FOX THEATER
660 Peachtree St NE, Atlanta, 404-881-2100
www.foxtheatre.org
The historic Fox Theatre is a mammoth 4,678 seat
theater that offers more than 300 performances a year
including everything from Broadway to rock n roll
performances. The 1929 theatre was originally built
as a movie house, but it's worth a show on its own,
and you can book a guided tour of the elaborate
facility famous for its Egyptian design themes run
amok.

GEORGIA AQUARIUM
225 Baker St. NW, 404-581-4000
www.georgiaaquarium.org
NEIGHBORHOOD: Downtown
Modest admission fee; buy tickets online so you don't
wait in line. **TIP:** do yourself a favor and go early, as
it gets crowded. To really enjoy, plan on 3 hours.
Within its 10 million gallons of water, this
Aquarium—an aquatic zoo, really—houses 120,000
animals representing 500 species, including 4 young
whale sharks, beluga whales (the white cute ones),
bottlenose dolphins and manta rays. **Dolphin Tales**
is a show that features dazzling special effects (and,
oh, yes, dolphins). Don't overlook the **Journey with
Gentle Giants** program that lets you scuba (or
snorkel if you're not certified to dive) with whale
sharks. This was the world's largest aquarium when it
opened in 2005.

HIGH MUSEUM OF ART
1280 Peachtree St. NE, 404-733-4400
www.high.org
NEIGHBORHOOD: Midtown
The leading art museum in the Southeastern United
States. After its $130 million, three-building
expansion, the High Museum has gained world-class
status. Notable is its renowned collection of classic
and contemporary art and award-winning architecture
by Renzo Piano. Collections consist of more than
12,000 pieces and include 19th and 20th century
American and decorative art, significant European
pieces, modern and contemporary art, photography,
African art and Southern folk art (on top floor).
Entrance fee.

HISTORIC FOURTH WARD PARK
680 Dallas St NE, Atlanta, 404-546-6813
www.h4wpc.com/
Atlanta's Historic Fourth Ward Park is a popular spot
and features a large stormwater retention pond where
there are ducks the kids can feed. A large playground
also for kids. The park extends from Ponce City
Market south to Freedom Parkway and the Carter
Center.

JIMMY CARTER PRESIDENTIAL LIBRARY AND MUSEUM

441 Freedom Parkway, Atlanta, 404-865-7100
www.jimmycarterlibrary.gov/J
HOURS: Open Daily
ADMISSION: Moderate fee, Senior, military, students, and children are free
The library and museum holds U.S. President Jimmy Carter's papers and material relating to the Carter administration. The library is actually a research facility and museum holding approximately 27 million pages of Jimmy Carter's White House material including correspondence, memoranda, photographs, film, and videotape.

KENNESAW MOUNTAIN NATIONAL BATTLEFIELD PARK

900 Kennesaw Mountain Dr, Kennesaw, 770-427-4686
www.nps.gov/kemo/

Hours: Open daily
This park contains a Civil War battleground of the
Atlanta Campaign and Kennesaw Mountain.

KROG STREET MARKET
99 Krog St, Atlanta, 770-434-2400
https://krogstreetmarket.com/
NEIGHBORHOOD: Inman Park
A could of blocks east of the famous **Sweet Auburn
Curb Market** is this popular 9-acre mixed-use space
is filled with market stalls that sell produce, goods,
prepared food, Southern-grown restaurants and a few
retailers. I like **Grand Champion Barbecue**, where
you can get both pulled pork and brisket versions, as
well as **Xocolatl Small Batch Chocolate** and **Craft**,
a Japanese eatery specializing izakaya, a Japanese
place that serves food while the real emphasis is on
the drinks.

**MARTIN LUTHER KING JR. NATIONAL
HISTORIC SITE**
450 Auburn Ave. NE, 404-331-5190
www.nps.gov/malu/index.htm
NEIGHBORHOOD: Downtown
A National Historic Site consisting of several
buildings surrounding Martin Luther King, Jr.'s
boyhood home on Auburn Avenue in the Sweet
Auburn historic district, which for many years has
been the epicenter of African-American businesses.
The original Ebenezer Baptist Church is also part of
the national historic site that covers some 42 acres, as
well as Fire Station No. 6, and a gift shop. King and
wife Coretta are buried in the **King Center**, where

you can buy tickets to his birthplace. The Victorian house contains telling details that bring him to life. Did you know he was a champion player of the game Monopoly?

MUSEUM OF DESIGN
1315 Peachtree St. NE, 404-979-6455
www.museumofdesign.org
NEIGHBORHOOD: Midtown
Known as MODA, this is the only museum in the Southeast devoted exclusively to the study and celebration of all things design. Featured exhibitions include architecture, industrial and product design, interiors and furniture, graphics, and fashion. Moderate admission fee.

NATIONAL CENTER FOR CIVIL AND HUMAN RIGHTS
100 Ivan Allen Jr. Blvd, Atlanta, 678-999-8990
www.civilandhumanrights.org
HOURS: Open daily
ADMISSION: Moderate admission fee
This cultural attraction is referred to as a "must-see" and "truly inspiring." A powerful and interactive museum that connects the American Civil Rights Movement to today's Global Human Rights Movements. One particularly moving exhibit demonstrates what black students endured during the "lunch counter" protests of the '60s, when they demanded to be served alongside white people. You wear a set of headphones, and when you place your hands on the counter, you hear the threats of the taunting whites that get louder and more angry and

aggressive the longer you sit there. There are other exhibits emphasizing the struggles of other minorities like gays, women in Iran, the disabled, immigrants, etc.

OAKLAND CEMETERY
248 Oakland Ave. SE, 404-688-2107
www.oaklandcemetery.com
NEIGHBORHOOD: Downtown Southeast
During the 19th Century, the "rural garden" cemetery movement emerged as an alternative to crowded graveyards. Oakland exemplifies this movement. Here you'll find the tombs of 70,000 people, including the city's earliest inhabitants, as well as rich families with big tombstone markers. You can buy a map for $4 that shows you who's where, including the unprepossessing gravesite of "Gone With the Wind" novelist Margaret Mitchell. Also note the nearly 4,000 gravesites marked "CSA," which stands for Confederate States Army.

PIEDMONT PARK

1320 Monroe Dr NE, Atlanta, 404-875-7275
www.piedmontpark.org
NEIGHBORHOOD: Virginia Highland
A 189-acre urban park that features miles of paved
paths available for walking, running, biking and
inline skating. Popular destination for weekend
picnics. Picnic shelters, tables, benches and grills
available throughout the park. Play area for children
located near 12th Street Gate. Recreational areas
available include: 12 lighted tennis courts, two
softball fields, two soccer fields, two beach volleyball
courts and swimming center. The park also has a lake
where you can fish. The park hosts a variety of annual
celebrations and events including: Atlanta Pride
Festival, Screen on the Green film series, the Atlanta
Jazz Festival, the Atlanta Dogwood Festival, Georgia
Shakespeare Festival, Music Midtown, and Festival
Peachtree Latino.

STONE MOUNTAIN

1000 Robert E. Lee Blvd., Stone Mountain; 800-401-
2407
www.stonemountainpark.com
NEIGHBORHOOD: Half-hour east of Atlanta
A quartz monzonite dome monadrock known for the
enormous bas-relief on its north face, the largest bas-
relief in the world. The carving depicts three figures
of the Confederate States of America: Stonewall
Jackson, Robert E. Lee and Jefferson Davis. The
summit of the mountain can be reached by a walk-up
trail on the west side or by the Skyride aerial tram.

They also have a ropes course out here for serious climbers.

WOODRUFF ARTS CENTER
1280 Peachtree St NE, Atlanta, 404-733-4200
https://www.woodruffcenter.org
NEIGHBORHOOD: Downtown
ADMISSION varies per event
This is one of the largest arts center in the world and home to the Tony Award-winning Alliance Theatre, the Grammy Award-winning Atlanta Symphony Orchestra and the High Museum of Art, the leading art museum in the Southeast. This is a major visual and performing arts center. (The Woodruff in the name is for Robert Woodruff, who made his fortune in Coca-Cola.)

WORLD OF COCA-COLA MUSEUM

121 Baker St. NW, 404-676-5151

www.worldofcoca-cola.com

NEIGHBORHOOD: Downtown

Here you'll learn everything about Coke you ever wanted to know (and probably a whole lot more). Permanent exhibition tells the history of the Coca-Cola Company. They'll even show you the vault where they keep the secret recipe. Here you can try more than 60 products made by the company. (These are from all over the world, and you'll be surprised how much there is to see in this place. Try Manzana Lift sold in Chile or the drink Beverly marketed in Italy that has a bitter, bitter, bitter taste.) Moderate admission fee.

Chapter 8
SHOPPING & SERVICES

AMERICASMART
240 Peachtree St, NW, 800-ATL-MART
www.americasmart.com/
NEIGHBORHOOD:
AmericasMart is comprised of four buildings that are
open **to trade only**: the Atlanta Gift Mart, Atlanta
Merchandise Mart, Atlanta Apparel Mart and
Inforum. Each year, AmericasMart hosts more than

400,000 retailers from every state and more than 70 countries around the world in 17 home furnishings, gift, floor covering and apparel markets.

ATLANTA MADE
1187 Howell Mill Rd NW, Atlanta, 855-285-6233
www.atlantamade.us
NEIGHBORHOOD: East Atlanta
A unique showroom that only sells products designed and made in the Atlanta metro area, representing some 70 local craftsmen and their paintings, photographs, furniture, jewelry, sculptures, interesting ceramic pieces, and skin care products and even dog treats.

ATLANTA VISION OPTICAL
1215 Caroline St., Suite H 100, 404-522-8886
AtlVisionOptical.com

NEIGHBORHOOD: Near Inman Park and Candler Park.

Exclusive high-end eyewear is available from very unique lines from around the world. VIP room available for exclusive clients with very high-end eyewear. The owner has her own eyewear line that consists of unique materials such as leather, gold, white gold and water buffalo horn.

BILLY REID
1170 Howell Mill Rd. NW, 404-994-3144
www.billyreid.com
NEIGHBORHOOD: Westside

Westside Provisions District, connected to the similarly red-bricked **Westside Urban Market** by a bridge you walk across.

This area used to be known for abandoned mills, stockyards and warehouses until recent renovations brought in some of the best shopping in town. Designer Billy Reid's 2,500 square-foot place offers both men's and women's collections. The store also includes signature antique aesthetic, complete with vintage photographs, salvaged wood, old-fashioned furniture, flea-market finds and Southern-themed wall coverings. (The Westside Provisions District is a group of shops and boutiques housed in what used to be a meatpacking facility.)

BUCKHEAD VILLAGE DISTRICT
3035 Peachtree Rd, Atlanta, 404-939-9270
www.buckheadvillagedistrict.com

An outdoor shopping area boasting a unique collection of shops and restaurants. The 8-acre complex took about a decade to complete. Some of the shops include **Shake Shack** (Georgia's first location), **Billy Reid, Brunello Cucinelli, Christian Louboutin, Dior, Hermes, Jimmy Choo, American Cut, Southern Gentlemen,** and **Le Bilboquet.**

CACAO CAFÉ
1046 N Highland Ave NE, 404-892-8202 – Virginia-Highlands
CACAO
202 Permalume Place, 404-221-9090
www.cacaoatlanta.com
2 locations
Handcrafted chocolates at their best. This is a "bean-to-bar" chocolate maker, producing every chocolate product from the cocoa bean. Chocolate-dipped fruit, handmade truffles. (The "Italian Cowboy" is made with espresso and bourbon.) Great gifts.

CNN CENTER
www.cnn.com/tour/
190 Marietta St NW, 404-827-2300
NEIGHBORHOOD: Downtown
It's easy to buy tickets online. Or see **Atlanta CityPass**. The atrium at the entrance of the CNN Center offers a few gift shops on the lower level. A great spot for buying souvenirs that display Georgia and TBS network logo merchandise, including CNN, HLN and Cartoon Network characters at the CNN Store.

FARMERS MARKETS
In **Buckhead** you'll find the **Peachtree Road Farmers Market**
2744 Peachtree Rd NW, 404-365-1105
www.peachtreeroadfarmersmarket.com
It has great produce, made-to-order crepes, wood-fired pizzas. The booths are arranged in a large oval shape so you can walk through the inside ring and then the outside. In the **Poncey-Highland** area, try out the **Freedom Farmers' Market at the Carter Center** – www.freedomfarmersmkt.com - a smaller market, but lots of fun. In the **Morningside – Lenox Park** area, go to the **Morningside Farmers' Market** – www.morningsidemarket.com - this is the only market that's open year-round. It was the first to go all-organic. Only has about 15 vendors, but it's plenty.

LENOX SQUARE MALL
3393 Peachtree Rd. NE, 404-233-6767
www.simon.com/mall/lenox-square
NEIGHBORHOOD: buckhead
Across from **Phipps Plaza** and anchored by Neiman
Marcus, Bloomingdale's and Macy's, this mall is a
popular mall for chain-store shopping in Atlanta.
Stores include upscale Hermes, Burberry, Louis
Vuitton, Cartier and David Yurman, mid-high range
stores like Kate Spade, Coach and Polo, mid-range
stores like Banana Republic, Kenneth Cole, J. Crew,
Abercrombie, Aldo and Urban Outfitters, and a few
mid-low range stores such as the Gap. Also has a
large Apple store. Outside of and next to the mall is a
strip of stores which includes a number of boutiques
including Blue Gene's.

ONWARD RESERVE
3072 Early St NW - Ste 100, Atlanta, 404-814-8997
http://onwardreserve.com/
NEIGHBORGHOOD: Buckhead
Excellent store for upwardly mobile Atlanta yuppies.
It has the feel of a modern hunting lodge, with the
deer antler mounted on the wall—look for Southern
preppy clothing from dozens of designers: Cotton
Snaps, Castaway, Brackish, duck Head, Barbour,
Dubarry, Peter Millar, southern Proper. Outerwear,
shirts, pants, jewelry—a vast array of clothing for
men.

PHIPPS PLAZA MALL
3500 Peachtree Rd NE, 404-262-0992
www.simon.com/
NEIGHBORHOOD: Buckhead
Anchored by Saks Fifth Avenue, Nordstrom and
Belk, this upscale mall has higher-end chain stores
such as Barney's Co-op, Intermix, Versace, Armani,
Gucci, Jimmy Choo and Tiffany's, including the only

Jeffrey store outside of New York, as well as an
AMC movie theater.

PONCE CITY MARKET
675 Ponce de Leon Ave, Atlanta, 404-900-7900
www.poncecitymarket.com
NEIGHBORHOOD: Buckhead
Ponce City Market breathes new life into the historic
Sears, Roebuck & Co. building in Atlanta. The classic
structure, which is the area's largest adaptive reuse
project, has been reinvented as a vibrant community
hub that houses Central Food Hall, various shops,
flats and offices, all while pointing back to the roots
of its inception. Only a few stores were open at press
time, including **Onward Reserve**, **Anthropologie**
and **West Elm**, but there's a LOT more to come,
believe me.

SID AND ANN MASHBURN
1198 Howell Mill Rd., 404-350-7132
www.annmashburn.com
www.sidmashburn.com
NEIGHBORHOOD: **Westside Urban Market** (next
to the Westside Provisions District)
Sid and Ann share the same location, but offer
different lines. The men's clothing shop offers
everything from socks to suits. The women's shop
boasts a classic approach to dressing a woman
offering everything from blouses and dresses to
jewelry, shirtdresses, pencil & wrap skirts.

SWEET AUBURN CURB MARKET
209 Edgewood Ave SE, Atlanta, 404-659-1665

www.thecurbmarket.com

NEIGHBORHOOD: Downtown

"USA Today" ranked this place as the 16th best food market in the world. It houses 24 independently-owned businesses from eateries to retail shops. There are plenty of places to eat fried chicken in Atlanta, so maybe you should skip the excellent chicken at the **Metro Deli Soul Food** hot bar, and opt instead for something a little different like Venezuelan arepas or the really nice and spicy Jamaican meat patties. One of my favorites is **Panbury's Double Crust Pies**, where the South African owners have adapted the pie concept so popular in their homeland to Atlanta, which explains why I like their Southern Breakfast Pie so much (with eggs, chicken sausage, and maple syrup). Other standouts are their Cajun Chicken Gumbo Pie with chicken, Andouille sausage, and Cajun spices, and the Cracked-Black-Pepper Steak Pie made with slow-braised beef shoulder and gravy. **Grindhouse Killer Burgers**, which has a couple of other locations in Atlanta, is here, too.

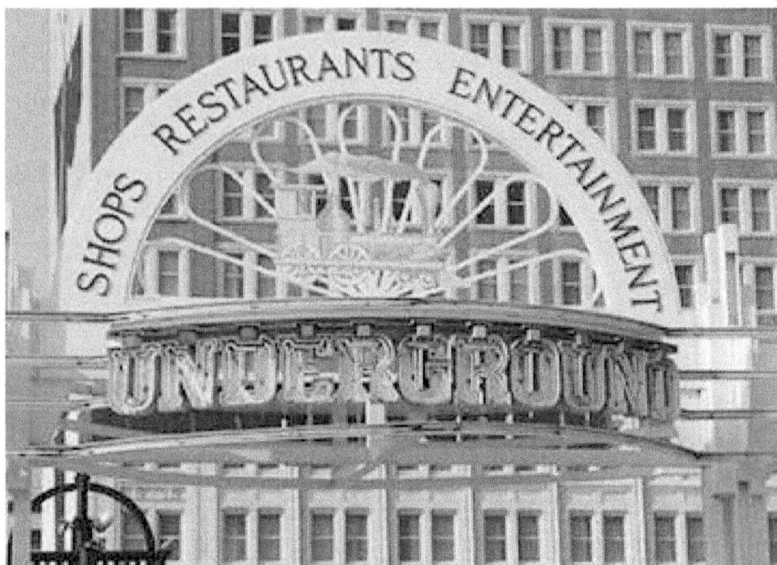

UNDERGROUND ATLANTA
www.underground-atlanta.com/
50 Upper Alabama St., 404-523-2311
Customer service center, 404-523-2311 ext. 7019
NEIGHBORHOOD: Downtown
Whether you want to shop, go to a bar, enjoy some varied nightlife or want to go eat, Underground Atlanta is a place where you can do it all. This popular tourist attraction is literally underground and is close to other downtown attractions such as the **World of Coca-Cola** and the **Georgia Aquarium**. Tour and local attraction tickets are available for purchase at several kiosks in the Underground, as well as shopping at a variety of unique retail stores. Located in the heart of the downtown, Underground Atlanta is one of the city's favorite attractions and a cultural hub. Opened in 1969 as a "city beneath the

streets," Underground Atlanta still exhibits many of the significant architectural features from its original structure. Visitors can pick up a self-guided history tour brochure at the information booth and discover the history firsthand. Explore six city blocks, 12 acres and three levels of 225,000 square feet of shopping, restaurants and entertainment at Underground Atlanta, a destination with more than 100 years of history.

VINO VENUE
4478 Chamblee Dunwoody Rd., 770-668-0435
www.atlantawineschool.com/
Want to learn more about wine? Here's the place, but

if you're just visiting, stop by this 4,000 square foot emporium to taste from among 50 bottles. Wine bar, food items as well as shopping.

WESTSIDE PROVISIONS DISTRICT
1100 Howell Mill Rd. NW, 404-815-0045
www.westsidepd.com
NEIGHBORHOOD: West Midtown
The district is a center of shopping and dining with a variety of retail boutiques and award-winning restaurants. Restaurants include: Bacchanalia, West Egg Café,
Taqueria del Sol, JCT. Kitchen & Bar, and Ormsby's. Shopping spots include Star Provisions, a gourmet shop.

INDEX